Black Loam

Also by Maxine Scates

Toluca Street

Holding Our Own: The Selected Poems of Ann Stanford
(Edited with David Trinidad)

Black Loam

Maxine Scates (signature)

Poems by Maxine Scates

Cherry Grove Collections

Published by Cherry Grove Collections
P.O. Box 541106
Cincinnati, OH 45254-1106

Typeset in Charter by WordTech Communications LLC,
Cincinnati, OH

ISBN: 1932339736
LCCN: 2004109488

Poetry Editor: Kevin Walzer
Business Editor: Lori Jareo

Visit us on the web at www.cherry-grove.com

Acknowledgments

Grateful acknowledgment to the editors of the journals in which the following poems originally appeared, sometimes in earlier versions.

Agni: "A Story"

American Poetry Review: "Fear"

Bloomsbury Review: "The Roses" and "Mother's Closet"

Crab Orchard Review: "The River"

Crazyhorse: "Wildness," "November Afternoon," "When the Angel Left," "Poppies," and "A Visit"

Cream City Review: "For Loss"

Hubbub: "Star-Isle," "The Mothers" and "Black Pearl"

Jefferson Monthly: "The Odds"

Luna: "Touch," "At the Veterans Home in Napa Valley" and "My Goat" (also reprinted in the online journal *Born)*

Massachusetts Review: "Deathbed" and "Wounded"

North American Review: "Adultery"

Northwest Review: "Still Life"

Poetry East: "Forgiveness"

Prairie Schooner: "The Swarm" and "The Curtain"

Quarterly West: "Green Pool"

Sycamore Review: "Drunk" appeared in an earlier version as "Leaping"

Willow Springs: "The Current"

The Women's Review of Books: "Sweet"

ZYZZYVA: "The Field"

I am grateful to the Oregon Arts Commission and Oregon Literary Arts for fellowships that supported the writing of these poems.

My gratitude goes to Lori Jareo and Kevin Walzer at WordTech; to Maggie Anderson, Hannah and Dan Goldrich, Kathleen Karlyn and Dennis Hartley, Lesli Larson and Sara Tripodi, Michele Piso, and Danna Schaeffer, for each of your sustaining ways; to Lucy Scates for what you continue to teach me; to Linda Sherman for your willingness to mine the depths; to Brigit Kelly, Dorianne Laux and Joseph Millar for your faith and editorial advice across long and short distances; and to Bill Cadbury—all thanks for the poetry of thirty springs.

For Bill

Contents

I.

The Making of a Medieval Book.....................13

Still Life.....................16

The Roses.....................18

Star-Isle.....................20

The Wilderness.....................22

The Odds.....................24

Fear.....................26

Black Pearl.....................28

Wounded.....................30

II.

For Loss.....................37

Green Pool.....................39

Wildness.....................41

November Afternoon.....................43

My Goat.....................45

Pain Comes Back.....................48

The Current.....................50

At the Veterans Home in Napa Valley.....................52

A Visit.....................55

Yellow Dog.....................58

The Curtain.....................60

Deathbed.....................62

III.

Luminous.....................67

Sweet.....................70

The Swarm.....................71

Touch.....................73

When the Angel Left...75
The River...77
Mother's Closet...79
The Field...81
When the Angel Came Back....................................83
Drunk..85

IV.
Forgiveness 89
Adultery 92
The Mothers..94
Spring...100
Poppies...101
Birds Flying Through 103
A Story..106
Soul Speaks...109
Goodbye..111

Notes...115
About the Author 116
About the Artist..117

I.

The Making of a Medieval Book

Parchment

Vellum, the animal's skin, most
prized a stillborn goat, soaked in lime
which loosened the fur, skin scraped
and scraped again, stretched to its taut limit—
an exacting art in a brutal age when arms and legs
stretched on a wheel, the body torn,
disjointed. They ate the animal, wrote
on its translucent skin, laid down their images
of backlit saints and angels and yet that skin
was still a veil across the face
they could not look upon.

Writing

The scribe wrote with a quill pen,
the feather of a goose or swan, a precise split
allowed the ink to flow. So many questions,
why the dying, why so many dead? The days
unfurled, a scythe slicing its way in a field of wheat,
voles and rabbits dead or scurrying, the as yet
unnamed violet-green swallow darting
in a swale of lilies. The book held the questions,
Azazel in the desert with his goat
his exile, the questions asked
of a single source, why shoals of bees
drawn to lavender, why the father fouling himself,
robe fallen open in his drunkenness, why archers

in the field, one tribe against another, and if
the wounds closed, what did the wounding
give birth to? They asked and when there was no answer,
they wrote the echo of that silence, harrowing,
raking across the yellow field.

Illumination

Bole, refined red clay and gum ammoniac,
sap, received the gold leaf and the silver
of the shiny surface. The coloring
derived from earth pigment: green earth, yellow
and red ochre; from the mineral: lapis lazuli,
malachite, azurite; from chemical: copper verdigris,
red and lead white; from organic: saffron, turnsole
and brazilwood. Here the incandescence,
their exultant vision, a god who might convince
with beauty and overcome even their own doubts,
and here a dangerous shining, the clapper of a bell
clanging matins on a still morning, thrushes
along the river underbrush, gave rise
to something else as some accepted exile:
the heretical alchemist boiled it down to one stone,
carts of dead jostled on the road, some followed
questions which had no answers, some followed beauty
numinous, living its own life, had fallen in love
with color, the precious metals of their haloes,
some with naming, red ochre, lapis lazuli, malachite,
turnsole and saffron, as if it were the light behind
the light, the only glimpse behind the veil
they'd ever have, and wasn't it?

Binding

Folded, gathered into groups called gatherings,
sewn into cords, laced to wooden boards
covered with leather. Book opening, book born
out of deference to a god, book born of fear,
of praise, book born of beauty, dangerous book
born of unanswerable questions, book born
of gold leaf and burning, book born
of wandering exile, of its own knowledge,
this making, this lure.

Still Life

Back bent to labor
Head bent to tears. . .
I'm drawn to Seurat's "The Stone Breaker,"
the faceless figure bending
torque of the body
twisting in acknowledgment:
no life beyond the life
in the field hammering rock
amidst yellow sheaves of light,
beautiful
because we know nothing of its grief.

In the bare bulbed kitchen
my father sat at the yellow table crying,
head in his hands,
because someone had reported him
for drinking at work.
My mother stood,
leaning toward him
with what sympathy she had left.
I wanted the light to settle on them
because together they were rarely still,
to make them so tired of the trouble
they caused they would lie down together spent,
and one summer evening in the heat
it seemed they finally had:

All of what I know of touch,
or grief or hopelessness,
springs from this moment

when I watch them from the window
their shapes muted by the glow of the street lamp
through the gritty screen—
their low stars the landing lights
of planes gliding the flight path,
engines drowning their voices.

He drinks slowly from his brown bottle
still somewhere this side of sanity
as they survey the patch of grass,
the maple tree straddling the curb,
but then the blur,
the heft and weight
of his arm grazing her side,
lifting to encircle her shoulder
and lower her prone to the grass,
the moment almost gentle
with the natural force of gravity
and as quickly
only weight slurred by insistence,
her refusal angering him
so suddenly he's in the kitchen
cursing her as he slams the ice box door.

She's outside alone, back bent
head bent, faceless,
safe, as night dissolves.

The Roses

What does my knowing mean for the rose?

Rilke

It was reading of the roots,
their tenacious feeding,
that brought me back to the roses
of the backyard
where my father dug the beds
and laid a grid of irrigation pipe
in his best imitation of order.
Three climbed the chain link fence,
the dusky white bush stood alone
shored by barricades of loam,
the yellow, the red
stood under the fledgling camphor tree
living their brief domestic lives.

Weeds then,
peaches falling from the neighbor's tree
the flesh corrupt
dissolving to the awful pit
a man in dream who lies there
among roses, among maggots
tossing money—
I know you want it—
the bills are green
scatter like blown petals.
I pick them up put them away
a cut that does not bleed,
the parade of dogs,
dust and drying shit,

the years when no one watered
yet they withstood the glaring sky
our wilderness,
the single and double blossoms
unfurling as they leached
water from the neighbor's yards.

In my first impulse toward retrieval,
I'd carry the shears through
the overgrown grass and cut the roses,
swing back through the gate
cradling their misshapen intricacy,
outer edges dying
as the inner still unraveled.
I've brought them here,
deep red, the white.
Outside my window
the yellow climbs the fence
built against the deer
though wild roses grow outside it,
a sacrifice to those who loved them first.

Star-Isle

When the gods first looked down
they saw our sea as sky, our islands, stars,
so far away thousands of light years later
we could only imagine their perfection.

The Catholic saints of childhood were closer,
more adaptable, even helpful, your mother
urged you to ask for help from St. Anthony
in finding anything lost, and St. Christopher,

patron saint of surfers swinging
from his silver chain, signaled who went steady
with who. Now, if you're still looking
for a god, some say

the encounter is in the unconscious,
that sea, everything outside the story
you've told yourself, everything
you don't want to know

clamoring at the threshold
where when you step through
each night you find an old woman
who lives alone stumbling toward death,

a bomber walking into the crowd, the mother
who pulls two shifts to keep her kids
in winter clothes, the speeding car,
a man driving his wife to the hospital

the soldiers firing, the driver killed,
their child born into a common nightmare.
Then, if you could look back,
you'd see the life you remember,

your waking life, that place of order, the star-isle
those gods looked down on, tiny in that vast sea.

The Wilderness

On the wall the openings: a photo
of the house on 97th, the dirty screens
and large mouth of the garage
where I sat in the coolness
with my cut head until the bleeding stopped,
a window I painted which is the window
I am looking through to the roses
tied to their trellis,
the archway of the church at Chamula
ordinary, *blue*, as the blue stone on the desk
though the other night I dreamt it in shards,
blue until the doors under the archway
open to incense and fire.

A stairway did lead somewhere,
a city lay beneath it which I sat above
some Sundays, the grid of order below
already yellowed. At home
I made a girl and stabbed her with knives.
All Catholic children suffer at night.
Days I was afraid.
On the playground walking through
the layer of rising heat a girl said
another girl had *scraped*
the white junk out of her privates.
I knew that meant something beyond bad.
I pretended I was lame and could not dance.
I did not understand the feelings in me
but I can see them in the Judas masks,

mouths gaping, placed
next to the empty maw of the garage.

I made a monster girl
who grew fat and snarling. I picked up
a hot brick and blistered every finger
of my hand and hid my hand. I had kissed
my father when he told me not to.
The lighter fell and burned the flesh of my thigh.
It did not bleed, the fire ate my flesh
and when the dog bit deep into my palm
I sought no comfort. I took my shirt off.
I had no breasts but understood
I was an animal. I ate food
other children threw into the street.
I peed for pennies in David's backyard.
I squatted, shat outside the bedroom window.
I wanted to be a river where nothing had awakened
where wholeness poured into and out of me
and what remained, remained untouched.

The Odds

The night I called my mother *obtuse*
I watched her turn to me
face flushed with anger as she said
Don't use words I can't understand.

I'm remembering as my father and I
sit on a bench at the Veterans Home
and he says thoughtfully,
"I might have been what you call illiterate,
might have forgotten how to read
if I hadn't kept reading after I dropped out,"
and I recall the stack of books
he'd take with him
even as he closed the bedroom door
on a Friday night for a weekend binge.

Now he's asking me the meaning of *tenure*,
how it works, what I might aspire to,
finishing a trade we began some minutes ago
when he explained *the odds* to me
because he's betting on the Oakland A's
twenty to five in the World Series—
our voices rising
because it's Veterans Day
and the Vietnam Veterans on Harleys
are circling this usually quiet plaza
revving their engines,
raising their fists to the older guys
who have come out of the wards to watch—
and as the Vietnam Vets snake their way

around this green enclosure,
I say, "This can't happen again,"
but he replies, "It will."

And I'm still thinking of that night—
both mother and I were just off work and Bobby,
the kid next door who'd dropped out,
had left that day for Vietnam. We'd argued
about the war all the way home and arms
full of groceries we stood at the front door
where, once in, she'd go to the kitchen
to make us dinner
and I'd go to my room to study:

I already understood the odds.

Fear

What am I thinking
when I stand at the counter?
I am chopping, adding onions
to the pan on the stove,
listening to music
and noticing
the days darken earlier now:
I am thinking of the body of a woman.

I am cooking
as my mother cooked on her day off
and what I am feeling
is her standing at the counter
and then she is moving around her house
as I move around mine:
I am thinking of my mother's hips,
the flesh of her stomach, did her body
loosen when she was alone?

And as I lift, turn and chop,
my hands busy with the air,
I can smell
the bleach from the cleaning
behind the scent of the cooking
and see her dresses ironed and hanging
from the doorframe:
I have entered that moving
I could not enter
when I came home from school
and opened the door to a woman

bound by motion
and I see that somehow these gestures
steadied the fluttering
that must have risen in her
as it rises in me now
when if I could I would call to her.

Instead I have learned to call to fear itself:
I have learned to name it,
the word she was walking with,
because as I say it
I can feel the edge of it
resist the end of the century
she bore me into the middle of,
and then I remember
this was the word my mother did not say,
it was the thing that rose
and fluttered in her,
rose and fluttered.

Black Pearl

The tiny lustrous pearl, a live bird's eye—
this eye was flat, depth gone, a frozen pond
the ant skated across, the bird's neck broken—
a Swainson's Thrush. I took in every detail,
dun colored wings, speckled lemon breast,
stilled song heard in woods lush with dampness
where rain reaches down to trillium.
                                        Song
that names a story I keep looking for
where a bridge arcs over a river a city casts
its evening light into. A man stops, hands
cupped around a flame, something seen then,
something passing, held—
                              I've looked for days,
can't find this story in any book I know. I stop
as my mother did yesterday in the Rite-Aid
parking lot, heat rising from the asphalt.
She doesn't trust what she sees—the sky is orange
pulsing with wings, and thousands of butterflies
flying north tell me this story is my own, one
early summer, weeks of rain, city kids so young
we had to walk into its endless flow. Rivulets
streaming we climbed a crumbling cliffside
above a river until we knew if we took another step
we'd slide into the raging snowmelt below.

We shouted, screamed high on our cliff,
day crossing into evening when they threw
the first rope down, when the boy I'd climbed with
kicked out and swung over the river. Struck

by falling stones, his body slackened, a tall boy
gone limp, blood on his forehead, head lolling,
light almost gone, but something held him,
his hands still gripped the rope as if darkness
had not yet traveled that far. Mid-air
his long body straightened, his head snapped
forward and he was saved.

Wounded

Tell me who has not been wounded.
                                        Miguel Hernández

We drove through the Ochocos
smoke in the distance, the ground
still smoldering. I saw it coming,
dreaming when the dog woke me,
already on the lakeshore, already fallen
before I remembered the warning.
Two nights later, drifting on painkillers,
the descent was pleasant, something
I had not forgotten. I said,
I have a little pony. I said, *You'll hate me*
by the time this is over. The afternoon
of the tenth, just out of surgery, my finger
on the button, I felt nothing, kept pressing.
I think Bill had come and gone, Joe
was reading a book. Annie stood
by the bedside. I told her about Italy.
I wanted them to climb the steep narrow streets
of Assisi, to walk with Saint Francis, doves
fluttering. The morning of the eleventh,
still on morphine, god of sleep, I woke
to the soundless TV, the planes, the towers of fire,
what had already happened, what
was still happening in an endless loop.

Weeks later we drove into the world again,
October, light bleak, washed, wan, flags
everywhere, pasted to windows, doors, waving
from car antennas. I remembered a woman

who looked at her husband, a man with secrets,
and saw a cloud whirling above him,
arms and legs flailing. I saw a heron flying
over a junkyard of rusted cars, an orchard's
windfallen apples, a child leading her dog
into the shade of a house and the beautiful gray
grain storage silo on the main street of Halsey.
Back in the armchair I wanted to know
about the gods I'd known as a child.
I read *The Aeneid*. I loved the honey, the bees,
his mother leading him to the golden bough,
how he listened to the clamoring voices,
how he crossed the river to come back.
I thought of the sprig of thyme from Crete
pressed between the pages of *The Iliad*
but did not get up to find it. I read Beowulf again
and when he slew the dragon the singers
warned him there was more to come. I wrote
down words from the poets I love, *harrow*,
winnow, sein, stubble. I wrote down *kindle*
which was hope, *hobbled* because I was,
rubble which was the world. I reread
a book which told how a cross becomes a weapon
and remembered the ashtray I made for my father
in the first grade, its red glaze, how the bits
of colored glass melted into the clay
when it baked in the kiln, how he threw it
at my mother, how I came to know anything
we touch can be a weapon. Listening to Schubert,
autumn hanging pendulous, a tear, on every note,
I crossed a campo in Venice, someone
playing a cello in an upstairs room. In 1968
in Los Angeles, days after Bobby Kennedy

had been shot, I stood at the front desk
of the Venice police station. I saw a man, naked,
handcuffed and shackled, propped
against the wall in a hallway. He had a cut
on his forehead, the blood had dried
and he could not brush it away. His white body
was creased by the fallen light, what I'd learn
to call painterly, abstractly beautiful for the body,
the light, so I would not feel what I saw,
the soul glimpsed, a man broken
by whatever he had or had not done.

In a winter of despair, the earth
cratered, strewn with flesh, I heard Bill asking
for a map of the world's rivers, the boundaries
of the natural, the waters that baptize
and dissolve. One morning
he called from the yard, late March,
wet snow falling. Wild turkeys roosted
in the bare maples. I watched them awhile.
I could tell when they were going to fly
because, draped with snow, they shook a little,
their feathers ruffled and the snow slid away.

I had two scars, one was fading. Sometimes
in the middle of the night the black current
of air carried the sound of trucks
downshifting on the other side of the ridge line
and I remembered how my father took me
to the stock car races, the monotonous din
of the cars running the dingy circle toward us
and away again and again, how, the race over,
we moved with the flow of men toward a crowd

surrounding an actor who had raced that night:
The air smelled of singed rubber, engines
roared and the planet whirled, already burning,
as we edged toward the actor, second son
in a TV western, little flame, but greater than us,
drawn as we were toward the light
that might touch us, the aura
which always dissipates as we approach,
the seal broken, the world rent.

II.

For Loss

The iris, the bird of paradise,
the trenchant rose all left behind,
bent avocado, black eyes of the mouse
escaping the stone incinerator,
smoke flowing upwards by the camphor
trees, our dreams
mixed with their roots. If I could see you
what would I say? And once I've asked
why should I be startled
by your presence summoned in dream,
you slip away through any net
that tries to hold you.

What remains
is testament to what might have been,
the abandoned orchard did not stop bearing,
we picked its apples near a town called Wren,
the broken shelves in the burned house
held mason jars of quartered pears
still spilling light, and the aged mother
hears her daughter calling out
long after the time for helping is past
because that call
has finally crossed the threshold.

All of us are waiting for the ferry
to take us across and as we wait
a small boy wakes in a hospital
after his village has been bombed.
He's told he walked in his sleep

and fell into a deep well,
rescued from those depths by the neighbor
who sits by his bedside. The worst
is worse than the boy can imagine—
the rest of his family is dead—
the dank water of the well
is the neighbor's gift to the boy,
truth will arrive in its own time.

Green Pool

I stand on the bridge
staring down at the green pool
eddying over the rocks
I can't see. I love its viscosity,
no reflection
but a place where light is troubled,
thick all of the time
blanketing whatever grows there.

I am not drowning yet,
just looking at the pool
though already it seems to be crying.
Now I resolve that when I speak to it,
as I soon will,
I will sound understanding
yet distant
so that its tears won't take me.

Somebody on the next bridge
could be trying to catch my attention
shouting
Don't talk to what
you can't see the bottom of. . .
but in a moment I will forget
and the pool will insist on its way
until each word means something else
until I think *Well, sure maybe it is. . .*
as the conversation we are having
pulls me into its not knowing.

Green pool.
It's the way a man in his small house calls out
when he is drunk and sad
and because he doesn't know which hurts more
finally screams *I am dying.*
He has to call it something,
but then everyone around him is confused
wondering why they can't see
what is killing him
until something begins to sicken them too,
a decay, they might call it,
a forest reduced to rotting stumps,
or if they are lucky
when they enter the room
they might say:
I thought you were a horse.

Wildness

The student surprised me
spoke to something deep in me
kept insisting,
You don't like me, do you?
Her words lawless
as a scene I once walked toward
on a busy street,
the rhythm of pedestrians broken suddenly
when a man's fist swung
into the face of a woman
walking toward him,
the woman falling backwards
as the man walked on
disappearing into the crowd.

Maybe the girl had never understood
there were things she shouldn't say,
yet the saying came as natural to her
as the man's crazed impulse to swing,
or so I thought as I lay awake all night
letting her words wash over me
defenseless,
assaulted as that woman,
wondering who the girl
thought she saw
until I recalled a photograph of myself
taken in an unprotected moment,
the lip curled, almost a snarl:
my father's face.

I'd never seen the resemblance so clearly
but the girl must have seen it
must have remembered
as she called to that wildness
waiting in me
as she said *Yes* and I said *No*
and she accused the girl I was
who taunted my father when he was drunk
too drunk to rise from the couch to reach me,
a game we played, were playing
my father and I, the girl and I,
when he'd say
You hate me, don't you?
And because I knew he would not remember,
I'd say, *Yes. I hate you.*

November Afternoon

The steam from the tar rises
past the yellow leaves of the maples
past the dun colored leaves of the oaks
as the roofers hurry to replace the roof
before the next storm.
The whole house shifts
shakes with the pounding,
the cat cowering under it
while I try to read
stroking the dog's big jaw,
hoping I slow whatever it is in her
that triggers the seizures,

and as I sip the bitter eucalyptus tea
meant to stall the cold from coming on,
I recall a story
a woman told me of her dog dying
one last dry autumn day:
She and her children had carried the dog
out into the yard and when they turned
to leave for school and work,
the dog rose and tried to walk to them
but stumbling fell. No,

when my dog slips between two worlds
I lie down beside her
talking to her as the minutes pass,
the center of her eyes clouding,
the opacity deepening,

widening in the paralysis of a gaze
that sees nothing:

She is running then,
the wet underbrush on the hillside
darkening her coat. I call to her
at the mouth of the dusky woods
and though she cannot see me,
my scent guides her through the brambles unscratched.
I hear her breathing as she approaches,
first the swallowing, then the panting
as she breaks into a dog grin—
as the house shakes, but does not fall.

My Goat

When the first goat appeared
I had forgotten I did not drink
my mother's milk. I was answering
a question from the dream about sons,
mothers and sons. Sad
because I had no sons, surprised
because I'd thought it was the daughters
that I miss. I'd dreamt the illustration
of a friend's poem to her son:
The boy was fearful. The mother
bent with him
larger sapling as if to sapling
absorbing him with a fullness
I can only say was knowledge.
There was a kind of light, a window.
I had forgotten all things
exist side by side:

the woodcut of the goat
on the cover of the book,
the goat beheaded by boys within,
and when a young woman heard that song
she'd found her voice in her own goat,
the bones of goats on the black basalt
of her childhood though when I read her poem
I'd been too busy to remember
the battered body of the goat I'd found
fallen from a cliff in Malin, the horns,
the curly coat tangled in seaweed.

I didn't want to think about the goats.
I opened Rushdie and there the cloven hoof.
I closed the book. But the goats
had grazed at the end of the dream
where I'd stood talking to my neighbor
over the heads of his small goats,
pygmy goats, almost like dogs I'd say
except they're not, they're goats.
I baa at them each day when I walk by
with my dog. I stood talking
to my neighbor over the heads of goats
about my father's body.

Yes, he agreed,
my father's flesh was unclean
his sex was everywhere, a weight
and I was sad again
wondering what the point is of finding goats
without the children. I felt
that I was stealing goats
though perhaps I was afraid to own them
because I did see no two goats were the same.
So much to think about, knives too
which are probably thorns, thorns which pierce
the eyes and blindness which occurs
when wandering in the desert. . .

My father was unclean.
When I was young
I went into the desert with him.
I did not drink my mother's milk.
I drank goat's milk
and it was then my goat awakened in me.

Pain Comes Back

When I can't pull the covers up
and wake him to do it for me,
I begin to wonder
why I stopped taking the pills.
I'd dreamt of going to a curandera,
jars of herbs stacked and dried. I listen
to my dreams—maybe it had gone away
and if it hadn't, the pain I don't feel
as long as I take my pills, I wanted
to see how much I hurt. Now
nerve endings popping, I know,
though the question I wanted to answer
was why am I so afraid
of feeling pain?

Why not feel what I have
the way the woman does who stands
on the corner each day leaning on her cane
knees twisting from the same disease?
She goes to work every day on that corner
dog at her feet, rain or sun, mostly rain,
umbrella over the dog, to show us
how much she hurts,
how much we don't. We wish
she wouldn't stand on that corner,
we don't like seeing her,
we think she should work for Goodwill,
we don't like seeing the dog
because if she didn't have a dog
she could live in a shelter—

but she loves that dog,
she's not giving him up
so she stands on that corner.

I roll down my window and give her my dollar:
Does the dollar feed the dog who lessens
her pain? I say *Don't stay out too long*
and drive on and each day it gets colder
she stands there longer, knees twisting
with her sign and her dog:
Disabled, Homeless, God Bless You.

The Current

If I'd had a daughter
I would have told her
about the child in the river
not my brother who floats down mother's memory
like Moses in a basket, is my mother a prophet?
Not Michael, bad brother, busted brother
of our same bad father. No,
I would have told her about the other child
who was floating away from Kafka.
Imagine being Kafka's child. A girl
in class asked how a bug could talk.
She was not listening.
Kafka was dying. He stood in the water
and let the child go.

And when she woke
she wore sorrow, a shawl cascading
as she rose from the middle of the river
though what she heard then
had to be forgotten,
a sound so exquisite, like
whales singing. The woman
played a recording, *I love the singing*
she said as I entered the room.
Twenty, thirty years ago
when no one was listening
it was their absence from the world
which made their singing unimaginable.

I would have held her.
I was on a train and I was reading.
I had no daughter. The train kept moving.
The cities were invisible. They existed
because of what we gave them.
The earth was opening. Someone
was selling lavender on a streetcorner.
Someone else needed to be buried.
He drove a horse and wagon
carrying a coffin. I stood at the crossroads.
I saw the other wagon, two horses galloping,
I raised my hand. . .we cast
olive branches in the open grave,
the crows were flying above the cemetery
long before we got there.

At the Veterans Home in Napa Valley

I'm cleaning out the room
he won't come back to, our photos
taped to the wall
with a copy of his commendation:
Fireman First Class fights
his biggest battle. Fifty years
later it's coming to an end,
and now I want his secrets,
a letter where he finally owns up,
says he's sorry with death's last flare,
but the only letters are those
he never mailed to the medal company
to replace what he'd lost along the way.

Downstairs they say he tapes
tens and twenties to the undersides
of drawers. I hadn't thought of that,
neither had he. The drawers are full
of stale graham crackers, cups of peanut butter,
hearing aid batteries and unopened cigars,
cigarettes. The shirts, the pants, smoke clinging,
line the closet. The many shoes of the dead,
a pair for every occasion, collect dust
under the bed. *We die and our things
are set out for the picking,*
he told me last year.

I take his USN cap
and walk back to the hospital past roses
blooming, the oak and eucalyptus sheltering

the cemetery up the hill
where no one's been buried for years—
expensive real estate, they ship
this village of old men and few women
elsewhere when they die. He likes his cap,
pulls at my blouse, wants me to kiss him,
unrepentant to the end.
I can't breathe, go talk
to Dorothy in billing who says
she loves my father, to the VA officer
Claude who says he knew my father
was somebody, knew he had a life once.

At five I make out the first sentence
of the day, *I want Mama to come,*
something elemental passing over
because she won't—
too many years, too much grief—
and then he's thrashing,
pulling at his tubes
as he begins to wail
Ma, Ma, Ma, Ma,
so loud the nurse hears him at her desk,
and when I ask, when the nurse asks
he points at the tube he wants gone,
the tube he knows keeps him alive.

He wants to die.
I want to sleep,
but first the phone calls, then
the long night and in the morning
when his doctor asks again
he looks up meekly. He's changed

his mind. He wants his tube to feed him.
I could kick myself. I believed him,
a kid again as he began
his death chant any drunken Saturday
at twilight, *I am dying,*
I am dying.

A Visit

Maybe he is with the boy,
bullet hole through his pant leg
blood on the snow,
the boy sliding under the fence
trying to wrestle free,
wrestle free of the inertia
that is his mother fallen from a streetcar
grown so large she cannot move
as he cannot move now. He wants the sun,
the mountains at Gold Camp. He wants
what glitters, the fool's gold
he reaches for in the river,
but now there are faces
calling him back and he is rushing
to the faces, the daughter
and the one he did not think would come,
who still will not bend to him
until he grabs her hand with his good hand
and pulls it to his lips
all of them crying
the father, the mother, the daughter.

This rushing, a confluence, a window
the daughter is looking through
when she is small, June bugs
batting the screen,
the man and the woman
lying on the grass on a summer evening,
the mother, surprised by memory
wiping her tears, the old man

trying to tell them all
he has been thinking these months,
raising his voice as if he believes
the importance of what he is trying to say
will make them understand until he sees
nothing will. . . He points
to the curtained window,
and sudden as that great rush
across distance he wants them gone,
sun pouring in from the curtain pulled aside,
from the window the daughter has opened,
he wants them to go, angry,
flailing at them until the daughter
takes the old woman away.

Later when the daughter returns
to sit by his bed he is quiet.
When she speaks to him
he seems to listen.
He looks at her even as he pulls
the gown up above his genitals,
the daughter looking away
from what was once a source of terror
until she sees he is only an old man
trying to brush a fly
from his limp cock where the tube runs out
and she brushes for him,
the fly buzzing in sunlight,
the little breeze from the window
pushing against the undertow
of urine and feces as the afternoon lengthens,

the old man thinking harder now,
brushing with his good hand
as he gazes out the window.

Yellow Dog

Of that day and this
so many crossings
in the span of your life,
on that day I stopped
and the next day you were born.
Yellow dog, that's what I called you
do you want to come home and live with us?

These last days
you led us to a new place, here
under the spreading walnut,
but I took you home
Let's go home
heart of me,
heart of the house
you found your way into.
You didn't love me much then, the pills,
what I had to do with your eyes.

Yellow dog, when the boy
touched you, you made of him a child
and *made of me*
who begins this twelfth year
without you, born tomorrow
that was it, we were born tomorrow,
up in the hills where I call
and you turn to look back.

Let's go home
and you lay in the road then,

the neighbors, the dogs came
and you lay in the road
while we spoke,
you went to the stream
of hot summer days only briefly
we dried you,
and then in the woods
you closed your eyes,
is she gone? I looked up
the last day of August, leaves drifting
already, your head simply dropped
and we carried you, the ebbing warm weight,
the big paws I touched last.

The Curtain

All that day
the man was dying in the next bed.
We never saw him, the curtain drawn,
my father and I on the other side,
the only voice between us mine.
My father could no longer speak
though as the morning wore on
he could hear the man's labored breathing
until the doctor arrived to ask him
if he wanted anything done
to prolong his life and he answered
clearly, as my father could not, *No.*

I heard the doctor tell someone
to write that down. I heard him tell
the nurse to call the man's son. They left,
the nurse returning to ask him if he
wanted something to ease the pain
of the wracking cough which seized him
again and again and he answered *Yes,*
the hours passing, his cough subsiding,
his breathing growing quieter
as the drugs took hold. My father's eyes
flickered in and out of sleep, my father
who could no longer deny anything,
who winced when I said, answering
the question his eyes had asked,
the man was very sick.

Late in the afternoon the son,
a grandson arrived. They tried
to rouse him, the grandson's adolescent voice
breaking as he said, *Grampa we're here*
though the man was beyond hearing,
the son saying to no one in particular
I didn't think it would be so quick.
I could have said something then,
how the man had answered earlier
how perhaps he did not know the drugs
would take him, float him so far toward death
before they arrived, but I did not.
His last day passed, my father
and I his silent witnesses.

Deathbed

He knew us
though seemed happiest
to see my brother, bringing
his hand up clenched
toward his chin,
and my brother who was a good son,
who handled social workers and VA officers
and gave him money and finally just food,
my brother laughed at the fist
though he did not when he was a boy
riding fast from home on his bike.

His hand reaching
the aide said, *Now he will drink*
though I asked the question
I had come to ask,
Do you want to die?
He cried then, his face sinking
into its mask. He was thirsty
but would not drink
standing there on the threshold
and when we asked, he nodded, *Yes,*
he wanted a priest,
he who had always stood outside.

Above the bed was a metal bar
he kept reaching for. He was so busy.
I lowered it and as if he were testing
he pulled but could not lift himself.
He wanted his hand held

and I had always been afraid of his hands.
I took his hand.
I said to my brother, *Look,*
his hand is as small as mine.

He did not want water but he was thirsty.
Death in his throat, he pulled
at the bar wanting to see what was left.
We said to him, *Look, Dad*
you have more hair than Allen.
We thought he smiled.
We went through his drawers
while we were waiting, nothing
was there. I didn't care.
I said, *You can go now.*

My brother went away for awhile.
I stood beside him. I wanted to tell him something
but could not think what it was.
Something protruded under his gown
and when he twisted
I saw it was his ribcage.
I said, *You are doing a brave thing.*
I remembered what I wanted to say
but was afraid to say it,
until finally I said,
Thank you for giving me life.

He still wanted.
He would not drink.
He was conscious. We said,
You can go.
Once he held two fingers up—

we thought for the two of us.
Each of us said goodbye.
On the way to the airport
we remembered the only thing
he could openly love
was the dog he'd named after himself,
the dog he taught to walk again
after it was hit by a car.

At the memorial
I said he healed the dog
but could not heal himself.
Then my brother stood and said,
My father was a truck driver.
He had a clean driving record
for twenty six years.
When I was a boy
he paid older boys to beat me up
so I could learn to fight for myself.

III.

Luminous

Yesterday I drove through the lush fields,
too much rain to plant them, sky closing
down over the tractors sunk in mud,
blue glistening black wings
brilliant red slashes of the red winged blackbird
rising from black loam. Twenty years ago,
my first spring in the valley, my car broke down.
Thumb out, I believed I was safe
until one day two farmers stopped to pick me up
and though I knew they'd been drinking,
the cab of the truck filled with the breath
of straw and Jack Daniels,
I could not say *No* to the ride.
Ten miles later I stood in the next town
knowing it wasn't my choice
but theirs, knowing I'd offered my life
and had it given back.

Crows caw in the mornings now
waking me, jays squawk in the woods.
I'd drive out in lambing season past the signless
Mennonite school, the girls
in their long dresses playing baseball.
Out there I taught in a two room schoolhouse
where the children came from dairy farms
their hands scrubbed to a blue veined
milky whiteness. Down the road
from the school a church
with a cross of daffodils planted on the hillside,
red tulips of blood spilling at Easter. Once

I climbed the hill to take a photograph
and found myself kneeling,
long grasses humming,
bees swarming past me into stacked boxes.

I had a friend who lived out there,
her house built along the river
which like our silences held us,
all day drifting in a yellow raft
following its course through the cornfields,
corn high and rustling, herons on the banks
wings lifting, the water flowing cool
beneath my back. One night
we walked up from the wide shore
where the water was low
the bank lined with stones
and my friend stopped to pull onions
from the garden,
clouds of Walla Walla whites
the air sudden with sweetness
as we swung toward each other
as my neighbor's children had swung
higher and higher through the clouds
of the blossoming cherry that spring.

Everything comes back to earth,
my neighbor's children are grown now
their old cat runs out of the field
when I wheel my bike up the hill
because the children once pushed their bikes
the same way, those wheels turning
echoing in the cat's memory
the way the walk from the river

echoes in mine: My friend's neighbors
nodding from porches,
heat slamming our bodies still wet from swimming,
the sweet smell of onions piercing the air
children scissoring higher and higher
something drawing us toward each other
hoisting us up for a moment
still ghostly, translucent in summer darkness.

Sweet

After the dying was over
when everything had been put away
when it came time to have something to say
no longer snarling behind the fence
could be
could be again,
the dog leaping in the field
beneath the blue butte
with the storm coming in
unsettling.

She found the mossy skull
of a doe and brought it to me.
This is absence
or so I thought
in the intricate sutures which had held,
the cavern of the eye
going back into itself and away.

Beneath the blue butte
the fences were fallen
the barbed wire useless,
who was I
tired then
in the muddy field
with the brown stalks
giving way to spring, who was I
if I was not who I had thought?

The Swarm

We trailed the cloud of bees
down the bare street of the housing tract
as the mother who did not work
leaned from her doorframe
shouting *Leave the bees alone.*
They came to rest in the skinny maple
assembling so quickly
we had to stone them,
the combs of honey falling
the bees without a queen lost
the scavenger wasps appearing from nowhere
to sting the dying bees
in the pools of honey on the pavement,
the wasps flying up suddenly as they did yesterday
when my foot plunged through periwinkle
into their nest
and they stung me as I ran.

No, that's memory's trick
then it was only a swarm,
something forming,
even as we threw those rocks reforming
intent on what they'd be. The hive
found its home in this life
lodged in our walls
suckling blackberries all summer.
The beekeeper came to take them
saying some would be lost
and it was then the wasps came to sting
the dying bees in the wasted pools of honey.

Then that I remembered for the first time
how naturally meanness
had come to us,
how one Saturday blocks away from home
we picked on a smaller child
whose father ran out to chase us
and as we ran I turned and called him
a *mother fucker* because I'd heard
those words at home
and understood how hurling them
things fell apart,
understood in the moment
before I ran again
in the reddening of the man's face
in his clenched fists
that he would have hit me
if I had not been a child
but instead stood stunned
not believing those words came from me,
why now I would not believe it either
would fly in the swarm
settle in the hive
and languorously fill each waxy comb.

Touch

Clouds parted, hands reached for us
because we wanted god made flesh
and flesh made touch
which cured the leper, forgave
the prostitute, raised the dead
from the dead.

In the outcast we saw
what might be changed if the untouchable
in us might too be touched
and in the risen dead, our deadened selves
cast off. Alive to the god in us
we hoed the garden, took the honey
from the comb, traced
simple designs of love—same god
who slapped the child,
held the knife to quivering throat—
our lot to wind and unwind,
do and undo.

And so the healers among us
reach hand for hand,
touch held between us each time anew,
what it might mean,
how it might change us
until it is its own body, flesh and blood,
salt of tears, our little temple
where fingers dip to tend the wound—
sting of vinegar, balm of tenderness—

until it seems again nothing festers,
the bloodied water finally clear,
nothing left untouched.

When the Angel Left

I have to believe the angel has left
before it can come back.
I have to know I do not want to be
here alone where the angel is not.
I have to know
that if I go fishing
I may pull up anything from the sea
including her face
which my memory does not want to love.

I never say the words
that she heard then
I do not want to know she heard them.
I cry instead at what I fled to—
beautiful lines inked on a page.
But when the words rise up between the lines—
cock sucker, cunt—
and in my dreams the little girl
struts red-lipped in her high heels,
I wake to her.

She tells me I am selfish,
I've come before only to leave
as free as him to come or go
leaving her alone with so much shame.
She warns me not to come back
unless I want to stay
unless I want to hear her story.
I call her *sweet marrow*
but she knows I want her to shut up.

She keeps on ranting. She tells me
her fierceness kept me alive,
I would have stayed a drunk or died
without her and so she rants
and so I have to listen
to how she hates the angel
who left her then.

But as I listen
I hear her say *I hate you*
and know she must be talking
to something she thinks is there
when I had remembered
there was nothing. I see
that for all she says she hates,
for all she thinks she should be punished
the angel does not strike her
and then I know it is me
who thinks she should be punished
the angel who does not.

The River

I want to lie down in the river.
I know that's where sorrow is,
sorrow the name I gave to a dog
long after she was dead
because I forgot to feed her,
forgot to feed sorrow, to remember
she needed to be fed. The wild cherries
glisten in the sunlight, the crows
clatter overhead
and somewhere the woodpecker thrums a trunk.
I know I could pick strawberries on the road
to the river, bend in the dusty rows
reaching for them in that moment
before sweetness fades.

I know the raccoon
lies dead by the side of the road
readying me, or is it these days
when the iris blooms as I want it to,
when the cat sits perfectly on her corner
of the fence? I know the flocks of redwings
are waiting there. They flash in the trees.

I want to drift all day in the yellow raft
past the corn in the fields, past the island,
the sweet grasses on its bank. I'll feel
the cool water coursing against my back.
No, I know when Sam Cooke sings
This world with all of its allurements
I want to cry. I know most of what I feel

is the fault of something else, blessed singing
or those full glasses of wine
though maybe they only eased the way,
or maybe I wasn't feeling it yet,
I don't know.
I don't know how to say it
though the body would, full of its love
its joy.

I want to touch you.
I want you to touch me.
I want to lie down where your arms
will hold me, where the birds
are at work riding the half-drowning trees.

Mother's Closet

This is everything she ever closed a door
on, the broom closet of childhood
where no one could ever find a broom.
Here, layer upon layer, nothing breathes:
photo albums curl at the edges, books
she brought home from the library
where she worked, handled by thousands
of other hands before their final exile
where they've waited, paper and more paper
taking in the ocean air, about to sprout.

Mother's sitting on the bed
with her tattered list of dispersals—who gets
what among the treasures she hopes
I'll find, but I know I'm seeing
what she doesn't want me to see,
the daughter cleaning doing what the son
would never do. After an hour of excavation
the console TV emerges from beneath
forgotten sweaters and balled up nylons
saved for stuffing puppets, a long ago church project—
the TV arrived in 1966 same day I crushed
the fender of the car, upsetting
the careful plans she'd made for payment.

She wants to leave so much behind. Hours later
I've found nothing I want but the purple mache mask
I made in the fourth grade. I like its yellow eyes.
She looks at each magazine I remove, saving
every word about my brother, the coach. He's sixty

and a long dead mouse has eaten the laces
of his baby shoes. I want order. I say
I'm old myself, I've started throwing things away.
I'm lying. I've kept everything she's ever given me.

The Field

The dog I had as a child
never knew a field.
She ran her beaten path
among fallen peaches,
among roses and dried shit
behind a half painted picket fence.
For years I've dreamed I forgot to feed her
though I never dreamed her dead,
she waited to run this field in summer
where you're laughing at the horse
who lopes in from nowhere,
where nothing but the field
where everything the field is
prepares us for each arrival
my dog running among the purple thistle
and vagrant daisies—
she who knows barbed wire
only because she didn't see the fence
so took the simplest route
and ran straight for me when I called.

Then *fence* was what she had to learn
so now she finds her way around it
dust from her paws rising
settling on the banks of flowering blackberries
in the same way
I'm learning to ignore
the peeling signs nailed to post
and tree warning against trespass
in a field no one could own,

opening into that spring
I'm telling you about when everything was color,
the depth of green I could not see into,
the red I loved before memory
when I rode my mother's womb,
and here I know you will speak of your own mother
before you speak. In this morning's dream
I bend to lift my mother.
She is so light
a husk who has fallen
yielding to me
we yield to each other
the way the long grasses of this field sway in wind.

When the Angel Came Back

I had traveled far that winter—
maybe I had already stopped scoffing
at the angel. I still did not know
what I was talking to and could only
speak to it lying down
which was the hardest part
because it came so suddenly,
the terrible pressure in my thighs
as something pinned, then billowing
rolled toward me. I feared if I told
what it was all else would give way.

I think you know this kind of fear
and what waits there on the other side—
unimaginable—though I can tell you
I'd spent years imagining
what it might be. But what
I know now was the angel
let me meet it, that burning,
that roaring,
my body a red sunset
coiling up from two worlds closing,
and then my legs were twisted,
and then I knew what *sinew* meant
wound round the thistle that was me
until one day I think
I screamed I know I did—
and when I tried to speak
I could not because I was far away
living deep inside the hollow of the bone—

I knew what had been hidden,
what I had hidden in the years
the angel gave back to me.

Drunk

For an instant I remembered everything,
those darkened rooms, the moment
between late afternoon and twilight
that deepening
as if I'd crossed the border
and come down from the Siskiyous
into the wildness: overgrown fields
and blossoming orchards
next to the interstate—
that sweet scent through the open windows
a thickness buoying me
until I stood next to the horse again,
a palomino walled in a shed
somewhere beyond the flat radius of streets.

Then I was a child, sleepy,
until I leaned into the opening
and heard the murmuring I'd hear years later,
the voices and the dreams
riding in the current of a golden horse—
I'd give it wings, that sweetness, that rising
I came to call desire,
the years then when I listened,
drank too deeply
confused by what I heard
forgetting I'd first heard it as a child.
And so I turned from a golden horse
in a field of weeds, or the huge purple
and white lilacs
which bloom each spring in the cemetery

tangling with graves and air,
reaching down and reaching up from what decays,
afraid of rising because I'd fallen
just as plums turn taut with ripeness
and unpicked let go,
split, wasted in the gutters of a city street.

What if now I admit to loving
the heaviness with which they fall
or that on a warm day in October I'm not sad
because the hillside smells of blackberries
past their time. The birds are happy, fluttering
from bush to bush, drinking fermented berries.
My dog and I have found the last apple on the tree
which I am shaking—love rides this current,
winter coming on, I'm drunk with loving,
knowing none of this was waste.

IV.

Forgiveness

All one winter
I drove the same road
and something was breaking up
something was drifting under me.
Each day I watched the flooded fields—
thin line of river in the distance,
gray blue of sky deepening on the horizon,
barns where horses
stood in each barnyard
breathing their voluptuous white breath,
some barns barely holding,
some gently giving in to disintegration,
and finally I saw
pieces of my life floating there,
risen in the flooded fields.

I thought I had pillowed my head on an island,
I thought I was dreaming,
gone, drifting where all of them were—
prowler at the window where rose petals fell,
drunken men on a swing,
blur of a murder misting around them—
though each time I'd seen them
I'd had no words for the dreamscape
framed by the rooms of an emptier house
where I had always lived,
the ground shifting and scraping
to a redness
as when each spring I'd climb the stairs
through the twilight

to find only the light above the red painting lit
and the gap would open
saying I did not know the painting,
or the house where I'd lived for ten years
or my life.

So I drove that road
and then one twilight
I saw the old woman turn her car into the sun
to watch one yellow light
drop into the river.
Or maybe it was summer again
when I saw the women lifting clumps of irises,
staking them, tying
the heavy blooms, those imperfect flowers
so full of beauty they broke their own stalks.

Maybe that twilight
or all those twilights rising together
like herons from the flooded fields
I began to know forgiveness,
to forgive my mother for the fear
that blocked her memory,
to forgive myself for the fear
that blocked my own, to forgive
what had died in each of us.

And even as I heard the voice say
Poor sad human being,
the hardest thing to give up was the hatred
when I stood over my father's body.
I still fall into the well of the house,
its sunroom, its stairs, its dirty kitchen.

I still fall into its redness
where those who were hurt
in turn hurt each other,
where we lied
because we thought no one else lied,
because we thought we had to face the world with a story
when there, in the house, was no explanation,
only the deep wounds and senselessness
and all of us falling.

*

One spring on that road
I crossed the train tracks,
I saw how the weeds lay down in the heat,
how the wild roses
tangled with the blackberry vines.
I knew I had come to love the stand of oaks
whose shape I could see even late in the evening.

They rise through me some mornings when I wake.
Rise through me
like the herons from the fields
with unencumbered grace.

Adultery

The cut office hours, kids sitting
outside in sunlight, spring, concrete

and cigarette butts, the grass still sodden
with winter, all the wisdom they don't have

and what little they know about themselves,
their own godliness, their own greed,

all falling away as the man at the lectern
tried to say something about the woman

he'd loved those afternoons, voice quavering,
birds tumbling in flight, seats creaking, students

settling. He was old, the pause seemed
almost holy, the late strings of Beethoven

hovering then answering, as if he would give
that long ago lover a gift, offer again

the moments before consequence, like those summer
mornings when having dreamt you so long

it seemed I had not yet awakened when you came
to me in the room under the eaves. Afterwards

we'd sit on the porch looking out at the garden,
the apple tree just past blossoming, the grape

arbor where the cat slept. I knew
you were married, but good or bad wasn't part of it,

not yet, maybe that's what the man meant,
the time between where we belonged to nothing,

still innocent, no one bruised, nothing broken.
Not until late in the summer when you left her,

when you asked if I'd thought what it meant for us—
not until then the scrim of dirty edges

I didn't want, unready, but when you thought
of returning I knew what I wanted. On August

nights like this one, the ballgame on low,
the dog asleep on the floor, I remember

how the light hung then, heavy, burnished,
the unpicked apples falling into gutters all over town.

The Mothers

Out the window a white horse
bent its head in a meadow, granite cliffs
the backdrop. You'd crawled inside a beehive hut,
dark, quiet, cold as a tomb
and understood the nature of the penitent's life,
lamb of god taking away the sins of the world,
your mother praying
after receiving instructions
from the phone prayer tree—
all she'd never given you, giving
it to god instead. She'd found you difficult,
but wasn't that the chance she took?
The mothers with you for a moment then,
those in the room, those left behind,
impossible umbilical of grief a lifetime
does not sever. You looked again
and saw the grass barely grew
where the horse bent its head,
the meadow little more than a rocky field,
so much struggle, sometimes loss.

You didn't know it
but you were on your way somewhere,
window, horse, field, hut,
all a bridge where you'd spend years
understanding how if being born is forgetting,
living a life is remembering
all you've forgotten. You'd begin
with the children you never had,
the chances you hadn't taken,

Nora and Joseph, beautiful Joseph
only a name, Nora's sturdy legs
as she tumbled into you, the mother
you would not be, those you never named
shriveling, suffocating or turning to dogs
in dream, other people's children born,
then graduating from high school
your own body giving up the thought of them
because you'd always known
you would not have them, you'd known
very young the mother walking away from you,
the mother you at first wanted to avoid
because you knew the old need
was waiting there bottomless, unknown,
bedroom door shut,
sign that said *Do Not Enter,*
the mother waiting behind it.

You began assembling all the pieces
of the mothers you had known,
a sort of world's body of mother,
palimpsest of mother, the layers
lifting away one by one, flesh
and death and perfume,
that illusive scent,
silk sometimes, Ava Gardner drifting
through the housing tract, the neighbor
who held you, her sorrow,
the bird she loved escaped from its cage
back broken under her foot,
armpit and drunkenness,
the fatted baby on the hip, the shitty diapers,
toys scattered, squalor of mother that was it too,

familiar tap of heels the mother walking
to the bus stop on summer mornings,
the long day that followed,
the mother walking home from work at night
arms full of groceries, mother
in the confessional whispering her sins,
you waiting, wondering what she had done,
why she whispered so long, blindered mother
who would not see, the mother in the bar
you are drinking with at twenty, confused
because you're too old to be her child.
You know there's something you want,
that scent, one last chance to burrow.
She tells you a story of a long winter
in the mountains, the breaking spring,
mothers and children playing tag
in a meadow by the river junction.
You want to be in the meadow, a child,
the teacher mother in front of the class
lets you say it in words, benevolent
white haired ethereal mother still smiling in dream
though wasn't she someone's mother too,
didn't she disappoint? She tells you to sing her back,
sing them all back, silk mother dying
and you hear the news in a phone booth
on the Rialto Bridge staring at rows of oranges
bright in fog.

All of them gather, the mothers insistent
while you sit in the room at her feet. She stands in
for all of them and she's not afraid. She takes
everything you have to hurl at her
gives it back shit spun to gold

as the two of you tunnel further and further:
You're running home from school your face
tear stained, streaked with dirt,
the child nobody wanted, not even you.
Such pathos—everything
you've armed yourself against,
but she wants you, she's listening,
matrix of mother, bigger than you,
part of you as you are part of each other
changing each other with each piece
you give, each piece you take
until you know nothing
is more important than what you never had,
the losses accumulating with you in hot pursuit,
shapeshifting mother whispering the words
you don't want to hear, *Don't walk away,*
the words you have to hear yourself say,
go on say them, this is your litany,
Please don't leave me,
I get scared when you leave.
Every time someone leaves
it's you leaving all over again—
and finally you think you've opened
the closed body of grief. You think
you're all the motherless women
you've ever known—until all these years later
you help her dress. Your mother, old now
one breast bandaged one unbound
blossoming suddenly, surprisingly
like your own, breast you both know
you've never seen, and she tells you
how she'd seen her own mother's breasts
only once, how they'd hung, pendulous

to her waist after nursing six children,
how she'd wanted to protect her own daughter
from seeing the same.

What was it she saw in the folds
of her mother's flesh? She was twelve
her mother was thirty-two her breasts hanging
and then her mother was gone to the wards
where she would live for six years. She was twelve
her mother was gone, maybe
she was part of the reason, her fault
her mother had been taken away. Loose flesh,
wanton body, the body was bad, breasts
she had suckled as you would not suckle hers.
She knew she had asked for, had taken
too much. Poor little mother
who hid her body, door closed, if caught
unaware crouched jacklighted,
hands trying to cover,
and if she had been held, if she had burrowed
into the folds of her mother's flesh,
she was shamed by the memory of her head
nestled in pleasure because her mother
had gone, left her one more motherless girl.

And now you think again of that morning
all those years ago, the window,
the white horse, the meadow
which was a rocky field,
the penitent's hut and what you forgot,
the mother and daughter at the next table,
the mother a little silly, the daughter, middle-aged,
leaning across the table to brush something

from her mother's hair,
such tenderness,
those women, mother and daughter,
colliding with circumstance.

Spring

The rain stopped,
the slender stalk
held the head of the tulip
breathing, balanced
the greenness rising in heat,
wet earth steaming
as late sun shone. I carried
an armload of branches
and dead ferns. A woman was walking
up the hill, a stranger
her jacket tied around her waist,
she turned back when the road
seemed to end. I did not tell her
I follow the trail
to the field where the camas lily
and wild iris bloom
though until they bloom one mistakes
them for nothing more
than long stems of grass.
I follow. I stop
as the cat skitters up
catapults from the trunk of the madrone.
When I touch the frayed bark
of the oak stump it falls inward
to the endlessness
of its black loam. Rain begins again
and with it blossoms from the cherry drift,
stones shining seconds ago
now dull with dusk,
the petals scatter phosphorescent still.

Poppies

I wanted the poppies
because it is August the fog lifting
on this bay. I wanted the poppies
because through the city flows the river
where we all gather on hot summer days,
because Saturday morning
the bulldozers ripped the rotting boards
and ripening blackberries, razed
the homeless camps along its banks,
because Saturday afternoon
when the young mother looked up
from her book on the sandy inlet
the river had taken her child,
because Saturday night
another eighteen year old got shot
at the AM/PM Mini Mart
across from Schuback's Violins
though we did not know when we paused
at the signal on Sunday morning
and I admired as always
the way their fragile unstrung bodies
hung in their shining rows waiting to make music.

I wanted the poppies
because outside the city
on the road that follows the river here to the bay
a car had struck a doe
down from the hills on her way to water,
because further on traffic stopped—
mid-day come to a halt

but for the sirens, a passerby holding
up a blue sheet so the medics could care
for those flown from the truck
onto the thistle of the embankment.

I wanted the poppies
sold in their roadside bouquet.
I would have honestly left
the dollar and a half in the cigar box,
but we were going the wrong way.
I only glimpsed their brightness.

When we reached the bay
I lay down to the squawking of gulls,
half-asleep, crossing into a bare room
where I had brought nothing
when the dog barked
and I knew it was not me crossing
but the way the trawler emerged
from fog just now into the sunlight,
something almost seen as the trawler
passes into fog again—
the sunwashed room
where I would have placed the poppies
in my grandmother's blue vase,
the orange petals, the white walls—
the trawler crossing the treetops now
waves breaking against its bow,
seen only once and lost again
each figure battling the waves,
their broken, their drowned bodies
for each of them,
these orange poppies in a blue vase.

Birds Flying Through

Their heads more rose than scarlet
their name an echo flying toward me
whirling birds and tree,
rose, yellow, willow
swaying further down the hill,
they settled in the oak—
tanagers on every branch.
This morning they appear
flitting in the shadows of the maple
as if I had invented them
or they'd invented me
to try to name this world
this soft body
so suddenly green I thought I was dreaming.

I was dreaming
in your house, was that your body
the flesh that loved me as a child,
was that the touch that lingered
or the warmth of sunlight
on my skin, their feathered breasts
flashing a yellow I was about to recall
as they scattered up from the garden
dangling worms or seedlings
from their beaks, was that your body
opening or the door I opened to you then?

Next door my dog is barking
her name is *Star*

though I don't know that yet.
I never know which dog is barking,
poor ribby dog
poor ribby pacing dog
who barks a warning no one heeds
who takes each blow into her body
ears bloody from the flies that settle
who cannot fly so digs a hole.

I opened the door. I'm sorry I left.
I'm hoping for better. I try to tell
this story I know so well
but between each floating phrase
I fall away to understory. There
the oaks have died because the firs
tower over them, their roots dissolving,
the room a body
through which I am descending,
though you're still here,
a darkness I can't penetrate beyond
until I'm in it telling you
what I know of branches
of arms, of hands that hold on
or try to push away. I thrash
from side to side. I thought
he would kill her
who was my world, this little story,
this atom in the world's body.
I left. I could not save her.
I wanted someone to save me.

The tanagers appear
in one oak rising in full sun in the meadow.

I can't explain
but something opens, another door
god's foot or blessing—
the foot the way we breathe,
the syllables of breath we name
the cells we are
which form the larger body swallowing me
where I awake saying your name
the always waiting
the remembered,
the way I knew the tanagers
because I'd seen them flying through before
sun on their yellow wings, their rosy heads
the sun struck moment winging through
which calls and calls,
which tries to speak
in the measure of the touch
that touched me then.

A Story

Yesterday our neighbors married:
folded cranes of many colors
hanging from the ceiling
as the wild spring was blowing
framed in the windows behind them.

This evening
I remember a bus once brought us
into a village square at dusk,
I ask if you remember where we were.
You do. We had come down
from one of the walled towns
where the photographs of fascists and partisans
were embedded in the thick stone walls
overlooking the green plain
and a thread of river below.

It is Easter Sunday,
a voice on the radio
speaks of the last weeks in Belfast
and remembering the Easter Rising
quotes Yeats to end her story:
A terrible beauty is born.

*

I'd been dreaming of the river for days.

How had I forgotten I lived by that river?

In the valley
where I have not been for years,
there is the rush of it,
the smoke that rises
from the settlement by its junction,
the road snaking through
the pasturelands of grazing horses.
All follow the river
while I lie in the long grass of its banks
falling into a sleep so sweet, so heavy
I cannot open my eyes
though someone is moving close to me.

*

There was the story of an ending
I told myself again and again,
but one day
something turned in me
to say it was not so.
No one saw the assembling
disassembling going on.
I was in a still place,
very still, mutable
as before rain.

It is late.
I am reading,
and you are beside me sleeping.

If I placed my hand over your heart,
I would feel the terror of its fluttering,
pulsing, brilliant as the hummingbird

or the minnow darting at the surface
breathing this life,
this river of thought and blood.

Soul Speaks

You lie awake thinking
you see me, one blue note falling away
in the night sky. Nostalgic
you remember looking up, clouds blowing
across the moon, a cardinal in snow,
your mother sitting in a clearing,
broken green glass on the sidewalk—
the moment you first knew
something outside of yourself.

But face it, most of life is the rest of life:
the mall, 40, 50, 70 percent off
because it's January, a recession
time for getting what you don't need,
American life anyway, the grocery store,
the broken jar of mayonnaise on aisle four
everyone stepping around it
while the kid who makes minimum wage
mops it up, days butting
against each other, the cursing in traffic
horns honking, plates shifting
until I erupt into glorious babble,
the speaking in tongues, your own holy ghost,
you flowing, head just above water
riding the rapids.

So put your time in,
watch the endless crawl of headlines on CNN,
temple of the complex made simple:
"Quick Vote: Is Osama dead or alive?"

Keep thinking of the lake, that greenness,
wondering if you'll ever leap
just that way again, water sliding
over your head, dust melting away,
tiredness gone. Meanwhile, it's time to do
your toe loops in cursive, one more thing
you've forgotten.

Your foot above you
remember your only joke, your man Achilles,
life hanging by the heel—by the waters
you, too, were not dipped, by the waters
you fell, almost mythic. Across the woods
a woman is walking her dogs, her foot lifting
over the log and landing cradled by green moss,
so many varieties of green, and sometimes
I come softly, *pale lichen,*
darker side of tree trunks, evergreens
muted by gray sky. I echo,
you've found me, once again.

Goodbye

If you died today, as many have, and one
among them, a distant aunt, you'd say goodbye
to nests swaying high, woven tight with twigs,
with string, with tufts of weed crown, goodbye
to something resembling a fat crow, a cat
its broad glossy butt resting in the crotch
where two branches meet. You'd leave
a redtailed hawk on a fencepost, two horses,
an appaloosa and a bay, standing
in a muddy barnyard. You'd leave behind
swans entangled in barbed wire
and the brown pelican washed ashore
with its beak cut off, the cruelty we bestow
on animals and each other. If you'd lived a full life,
say eighty years, as this aunt did, you were born
after the first world war. You lost a husband,
like all men in our family a veteran of the second,
to polio one day in 1952, raised
three children alone, endured, your life spanning
the many wars of the twentieth century.

You said goodbye before the first war
of the twenty-first, goodbye to sunflowers,
their woody stems high as light stanchions,
necks bent, ragged flowers frozen in winter fog,
the lone llama staring at the blue hills, the long necks
of Canada geese, the bright ringed mallards
up from the slough flying in pairs. And if
you are born into this moment as many will be,
know weeks from now clouds of bees

may still stumble among lilacs
curling brown with rain, red cranes
will rise, elegant against the skyline they build,
trucks will haul rooftiles and great trunks of trees
wrenched from the woods. Know trailers of canoes
slick with lacquer will ride the Blue Star
Memorial Highway, same blue stars my family
pasted to the window when five sons and sons-in-law
went off to fight a war we now call good,
and even so my father wept, saying he did not
have to kill those boys. Today in the city
the clouds have cleared, to the east the mountain
is out, white with snow, backdrop to industry
and hillside cemeteries. Today the river
is glistening, its many bridges arcing—
its bright cars shining ride into the sun.

Notes

"The Making of a Medieval Book" takes its title and its framing from an exhibit of the same name at the J. Paul Getty Museum in Los Angeles.

"The Mothers" is for Linda Sherman.

About the Author

Maxine Scates is also the author of *Toluca Street,* which received the Agnes Lynch Starrett Poetry Prize from the University of Pittsburgh Press, and subsequently the Oregon Book Award for Poetry. She is co-editor, with David Trinidad, of *Holding Our Own: The Selected Poems of Ann Stanford,* published by Copper Canyon Press. She has received fellowships in poetry from the Oregon Arts Commission and Literary Arts, and her poems have appeared in such journals as *Agni, American Poetry Review, Antioch Review, Crab Orchard Review, Crazyhorse, Hubbub, Ironwood, Luna, Massachusetts Review, Missouri Review, North American Review, Poetry East, Prairie Schooner, Quarterly West, The Women's Review of Books,* and *ZYZZYVA.* She has taught at the Mountain Writers Center and as Writer-in-Residence at Lewis and Clark College and Reed College. Currently, she teaches privately. Born and raised in Los Angeles, she moved to Eugene, Oregon in 1973 where she lives with her husband, Bill Cadbury.

About the Artist

Painter Dennis Hartley is an architect and furniture designer who in 1997 put aside other pursuits to devote his career to art. Registered as an architect since 1976, he apprenticed abroad in Lausanne and Paris, as well as with major firms in Los Angeles, before starting his own practice. His chair designs have been showcased at the New York Furniture Fair as well as in designer showrooms from coast to coast. He resides in Eugene, Oregon, and is currently represented by fine art galleries in Santa Fe, New Mexico and Lincoln City, Oregon.

Printed in the United States
29444LVS00005B/208-231

Beauty, fear, praise, unanswerable questions, wandering exile: these are the expansive concerns of Maxine Scates' tightly composed, musically precise lyrics. *Black Loam* is a masterful second collection for Scates.

"Maxine Scates' *Black Loam* maps the difficult choices forced upon us all—which wounds to deepen in order not to forget, which wounds to will into healing. In a world often filled with squalor and cruelty, Scates does not find redemption, but finds survival, and maybe finally that is all the redemption that's out there for us. These clear-eyed, frank, hard-hitting poems demonstrate a careful attention to the things of the world. Scates wisely knows when to slow down to paint her layered, textured images. She recognizes the penetrating moments that change our lives in an instant. Scates is there when the veil is lifted. In fact, I often feel that she is the one doing the lifting."—Jim Daniels

"*Black Loam* is a quietly compelling collection of poems, the steady pulse of which is the psychic drive toward maturation. Its obsessive return to certain luminous or devastating moments of childhood is dynamic, however, not prevaricating, steadily subjecting those crystalline memories to the powers of the now. Chief of these are mind and the intimate, almost personal apprehension of the natural world. The dark river that we—and poets—used to expect to swallow poets whole—brilliant, crippled children to the end—is the tow Scates rows against with every pull of her oars. *Black Loam's* poems are rich and disciplined, concerned with psychic landscape not as a naturalist or a photographer might be, but as the saving site of a mythic, strenuous journey home."—Linda McCarriston

About the painting: "Bird's Eye Barn" by Dennis Hartley, 35 x 25, oil on canvas, 2003.

Author photo: Bill Cadbury

ISBN 1-932339-73-6

90000

9 781932 339734

Cherry Grove Collections